Reflections on Nature

in These Times

by

Hieromonk Alexii Altschul

Printed with the blessing of His Grace

+ Longin

Serbian Orthodox Bishop of the Diocese

of New Gracanica and Midwestern America

www.theosisbooks.net

ISBN 978-1548063689
Printed in the United States of America.

Reflections
on Nature
in These Times

Reflections on Nature in These Times

"Treebeard rumbled for a moment... 'Only lately did I guess that Saruman was to blame ... he and his foul folk are making havoc now. Down on the borders they are felling trees -- good trees. Some of the trees they just cut down and leave to rot -- orc-mischief that; but most are hewn up and carried off to feed the fires of Orthanc. There is always a smoke rising from Isengard these days ... To land of gloom with trump of doom, with roll of drum, we come; To Isengard with doom we come!"

(*The Two Towers*, Tolkien, J.R.R., 1954, pp. 462,474. 2nd ed. 1994, Houghton Mifflin Company, New York, NY).

"He will take holiness as an unconquerable shield and sharpen His relentless wrath for His sword; and *creation will fight with Him* against the senseless."

(*Wisdom of Solomon 5:20*, The Orthodox Study Bible, 2008, St. Athanasius Academy Septuagint. Thomas Nelson, Inc. Nashville)

I was deeply moved at Tolkien's description of the Ents, the ancient mythical trees that were moved to wrath to protect the rest of creation, described in the 2nd volume of The Lord of the Rings trilogy. Then, one day in church I read the above mentioned verse from the Wisdom of Solomon and I thought of Tolkien's Ents. Creation will fight with Him against the senseless. Regardless of one's thinking on Global Warming, there are many biblical passages to indicate that nature does rise up during times when humans deeply defect from their God-appointed role of guardians and loving caretakers of the earth. The flood of Noah, the destruction of Sodom, the plagues of Egypt, the famines during the reigns of some of the Hebrew Kings, as well as the prophesied natural disasters by our Lord Jesus Christ in the Gospels, to mention a few.

I have heard it said that rather than these being direct judgements, God's creation can only take so much before these things begin to take place. Indeed, St. Paul said that "the whole creation groans and labors with birth pangs together until now. (Rom. 8:22, NKJV, 1992,

Thomas Nelson, Inc. Nashville). This is the phrase the Lord Jesus Christ used to describe the natural phenomenon associated with the end of this age: birth pangs (Mt. 24:8 NASB). Both verses have the same root word in Greek for birth pangs.

So, how are we as Orthodox Christians to view nature, the environment, the visible creation of God? Rather than this being a scholarly or exhaustive work, the following lines are meditations and reflections on this subject from liturgical services, the Holy Fathers, the lives and writings of saints, with some correlations from Native American and African American sources.

To begin, let us consider the echo of Paradise provided through the lament seen through the eyes of a deer in the sorrowful but hopeful lamentation provided by the recently glorified Serbian Saint, Archimandrite Justin Popovich. Here are a few excerpts:

I am a deer. I am the sense of sorrow in the universe... I am more sorrowful than all creatures ... Sorrow is my constant companion. Each cruelty is an entire death for me. Most of all in this world I have been surviving in the cruelties of one being called--Man.

Sometimes he is the death of all my joys. O my eyes, look through him and above him to the One Who is All-Good and All-Gentle! Goodness and gentleness, this is life for me, this is immortality, this is eternity. Without goodness and gentleness,

Saint Justin Popovich

life is hell. When I keep in mind the goodness and gentleness of the All-Gentle One, I am completely in Paradise. If human cruelty closes in on me, hell closes in on me with all its terrors! Therefore, I am frightened of man, every man, unless he is good and gentle.

I am beside a stream whose banks are adorned with blue flowers. And the stream is from my tears. Men wound me in the heart, instead of blood, tears flow. O Gentle Heavens, to You I tell my secret. Therefore I weep for all the sorrowful, and the innocent, all the humiliated, all the insulted, all the hungry, all the homeless, all the distressed, all the tormented, all the saddened. My thoughts soon choke up with sorrow and turn into feelings, and the feelings pour out in tears. Yes, my feelings are boundless and my tears are countless. And almost every feeling in me grieves and weeps, because as soon as it turns from me to the world around me, it encounters some human cruelty. Oh, is there any being more cruel and brutal than man?

Why was I cast into this world among men?... Oh, once--long, long ago--when I, in my dense and boundless forests, did not know man, the world was joy and paradise for me. But he stepped into my paradise. He--cruel, brutal and arrogant man. He trampled my flowers, chopped down my woods, and darkened the sky. And thus he transformed my paradise into hell... Oh, I do not hate him for this reason, but I rather feel sorry for him. I feel sorry for him because he has no feeling for paradise ... I have heard that demons exist. It is really possible that they are worse than men?

The birches told us: "We saw Satan falling from heaven to earth, falling among men and-- remaining." He, the one who fell away from heaven, has declared: "It is very pleasant for me among men, and I have a paradise of my own -- men..."

I have been listening, the blue sky has been whispering to the black earth this eternal truth: On the day of judgment men will have to give an answer for all the torments, for all the sufferings, for all the troubles, for all the deaths of all earthly beings and creatures. All the animals shall rise up and charge the human race with all the pains, with all the injuries, with all the evils, with all the deaths that it has caused them in its arrogant love of sin.

Oh, have mercy on me, All-Good and All-Gentle One. Oh, save me from men, from cruel and evil men. In this way you will transform my world into Paradise and my sorrow into joy...

More than all that I love, I love freedom. It consists of goodness, gentleness, and love. And evil, cruelty, and hatred--this is slavery of the worst sort. By being a slave to them, one is a slave to death. And is there any slavery more fearful than death? Men--these fabricators and makers of evil, cruelty, and hatred, led me away into such slavery.

Man invented and made sin, death, and hell. And this is worse than the worst thing, more terrifying than the most terrifying things in all my worlds ... With intelligence but without goodness and gentleness, man is a ready-made devil...

I have listened to the angels of Heaven, when they wash their wings in my tears. In ancient times the white deer told me that He, the All-meek and All-merciful One passed over the earth and transformed the earth back to Paradise. Wherever He stood, Paradise appeared. Out of Him unto all beings and all creation there would flow boundless goodness and love, gentleness, mercy, meekness, and wisdom. He walked over all the earth and brought Heaven down to earth. They called Him Jesus. We saw in Him that man can be wondrous and exceedingly beautiful only when he is sinless. He shared in our sorrow and wept with us. He was with us and against those human creations: sin, evil, and death. He loved all creatures gently and compassionately; He embraced them with a divine longing; and He

13

defended them from human sin, human evil, and human death. He was, and has forever remained-- our God, the God of the sorrowful and saddened creatures, from the smallest to the greatest.

Only those men who resemble Him -- are dear to us. They are our family, and our immortality, and our love. The soul of these men is woven from His goodness, and compassion, and Love, and gentleness, and meekness, and righteousness, and wisdom … They resemble the radiant and holy angels.

Therefore, all our love rushes toward the all-meek, all-good, all-merciful and gentle Jesus. He is -- our God, and our Immortality, and our Eternity... He--our Lord and God! He--our sweet consolation in this bitter world which is passing and our eternal joy in that immortal world which is coming...

(From *The Struggle for Faith and other Writings of Bishop Nikolai Velimirovich and Archimandrite Justin Popovich,* A Treasury of Serbian Orthodox Spirituality, Vol. IV. Second edition, 1999, pp. 144-156. The Serbian Orthodox Metropolitanate of New Gracanica, Grayslake, IL)

In Genesis, the Book of Beginnings, the creation of man and his relationship with creation is first mentioned:

"So God created man in his own image, in the image of God created he him; male and female created he them. And God blessed them, and God said unto them, Be fruitful, and multiply, and replenish the earth, and subdue it: and have *dominion* over the fish of the sea, and over the fowl of the air, and over every living thing that moveth upon the earth." (Gen. 1:27-28 KJV).

But what kind of dominion is this? In the Pulpit Commentary, reflecting a Calvinist perspective, the following comments are offered:

"The new-created race was intended to occupy the earth. How far during the first age of the world this Divine purpose was realized continues matter of debate (Genesis 10.). After the Flood the confusion of tongues effected a dispersion of the nations over the three great continents of the old world. At the present day man has wandered to the ends of the earth. Yet vast realms lie unexplored, waiting his arrival. This clause may be described as *the colonist's charter.* And subdue it. The commission thus received was to utilize for his necessities the vast resources of the earth, by agricultural and mining operations, by geographical research, scientific discovery, and mechanical invention. And have dominion over the fish of the sea, etc. i.e. over the inhabitants of all the elements. The Divine intention with regard to his creation was thus minutely fulfilled by his investiture with supremacy over all the other works of the Divine hand."

Thus, this commentary sees this verse as the "colonist's charter" to replenish and subdue. Yet, how did the early Christians understand this? The Apostle Barnabas in his *Epistle of Barnabas* comments on this verse.

"But He said above, 'Let them increase, and rule over the fishes.' Who then is able to govern the beasts, or the fishes, or the fowls of heaven? For we ought to perceive that to govern implies, authority, so that one should command and rule. If, therefore, this does not exist at present, yet still he has promised it to us. When? *When we ourselves also have been made perfect so as to become heirs of the covenant of the Lord.*"

(*The Epistle of Barnabas 7:8b-11*, Ante-Nicene Fathers, VOL. 1, The Apostolic Fathers, 1994, Hendrickson Publishers, Inc. Peabody, MA)

When we ourselves have been made perfect! The Slavonic word for a monastic saint is the word *"prepadobie"*, translated "according to the likeness" of the first-formed man. The image of Adam and Eve in Paradise has often been the model of what we are to return to, the original likeness. The kind of original dominion or lordship in Paradise is found in the way many saints treated animals and creation. Consider St. Paul of Obnora in the forests of Russia:

Saint Paul of Obnora

"Having heard of the ascetic labors of Paul, Sergius [of Nurma] went to him and saw in the forest a wondrous sight: A flock of birds surrounded the marvellous anchorite; little birds perched on the Elder's head and shoulders, and he fed them by hand. Nearby stood a bear, awaiting his food from the desert-dweller; foxes, rabbits and other beasts ran about, without any enmity among themselves and not fearing the bear. *Behold the life of innocent Adam in Eden, the lordship of man over creation,* which together with us groans because of our fall and thirsts to be delivered into the liberty of the children of God (Rom. 8:22)."

(*The Northern Thebaid: Monastic Saints of the Russian North*, 1975, p. 39, St. Herman of Alaska Brotherhood, Platina, California).

This kind of "lordship over creation" is an example of how the perfect is able to have authority over the animals (as St. Barnabas mentioned) as a loving caretaker, guardian and one who is an expression and link with the Loving Creator Himself. A more contemporary witness to this is newly glorified Saint

Paisios of the Holy Mountain. What he pursued and exemplified witnesses to the possibility of such a life. In the following words and story we have another witness to this kind of lordship of man over creation referred to by the Apostle Barnabas and seen in the life of St. Paul of Obnora. Elder Paisios wrote:

As long as Adam loved God and observed His commandment, he dwelt in the Paradise of God and God abode in the paradisiacal heart of Adam. Naked Adam was clothed with the Grace of God and, surrounded by all the animals, he held and caressed them lovingly, and they, in turn, licked him devoutly, as their master (Cf. Gen. 2:18-20). When Adam violated God's commandment, he was stripped of the Grace of God, clothed with a garment of skin and exiled from Paradise (Cf. Gen. 3:21-24). Grace-filled Adam became wild, and many animals, because of Adam, were also made savage, and instead of approaching him with devoutness and licking him with love, they lashed out at him with rage in order to tear at or bite him.

Today, the keeping of God's commandments once again draws man close to God, Who then removes his garment of skin, the old man, and clothes him anew with His Grace, being thus restored to his first state, before the Fall, Then, he moves about innocently among people and fearlessly among wild animals, which sense from very far away the innocence and love, approaching man once again and licking him with devotion, and, recognising him as their master, they cease to be wild since their master has been tamed.

O blessed desert, you who help so much in reconciling the creature of God with his Creator, and who are then transformed into an earthly paradise,

Saint Paisios of the Holy Mountain

gathering again the wild animals around man whom you have pacified!

Love, as much as you are able, the desert and incorporeal life and throw, as much as you can, your material possessions into the courtyards of the poor. Simplify your life, as much as you can, in order to be free from worldly stress, in order that your life has meaning...

Love the blessed desert (*erimo*, Gr.) and respect it, if you want the desert to assist you with its sacred seclusion (*eremia*, Gr.) and sweet serenity, that you may become serene and your passions devastated, so as to draw near unto God." (Epistles, pp. 203-205)

Saint Paisios sums up this kind of lordship when he wrote the following exhortation, echoing this ancient perspective.

Love with pain of heart for our fellowmen carries with it the power of Christ, to transform the souls of barbarians and tame wild beasts, which then draw near him like sheep." (ibid, p 206)

This kind of loving relationship between restored Adam and the creation is found in his response to a senseless killing of a snake.

One day he welcomed a pilgrim with a reprimand. "What have I done to you to hurt me so much today?" Everybody was astonished. "Father, this is the first time that I have ever met you. How could I have done you any harm?" the visitor responded. "You committed a terrible deed today. You hurt me deeply." "But what did I do, Father" "You killed my friend." "Your friend?" "Yes, my friend the snake."

"Do you see what happened? On the way to his hermitage these pilgrims had spotted a snake crossing the road and one of them killed it with a stick" [Elder] Paisios, being graced with the gifts of the Holy Spirit, saw with the eyes of his soul what the pilgrim did." (*Mountain of Silence*, Markides, K., p. 110).

When the Apostle Barnabas invites us to return to perfection, to the restoration of Adam in Christ, he presents an entirely different image from the connotation of a dominating, force-filled, rapacious, colonizing idea of lordship. It is important to note that the word for dominion or lordship in Genesis 1:28 in the Septuagint (the Greek version of the Old Testament translated by the top 70 Hebrew scholars 250 years before Christ) was the same word used by our Lord Jesus Christ in St. Matthew 20:25 and St. Mark 10:42. There He was contrasting the Gentiles "exercising lordship over them" with the greatest being as the servant, and the first being as the slave. This form of dominating leadership was "not so in the beginning." Our Lord is presenting His way of exercising lordship, that of a servant, a healer, someone that the deer in St. Justin Popovich's lament would feel safe with.

This kind of loving care for animals and nature is strewn throughout the Scriptures, but it was so much a part of the ethos that it wasn't often directly spoken of. Yet, consider these following verses:

Proverbs 12:10 (KJV) The righteous man regardeth ('has compassion on', LXX) the life of his beast, but the tender mercies of the wicked are cruel.

Ezekiel 34:17-22 (KJV) And as for you, O my flock, thus saith the Lord God; Behold, I judge between cattle and cattle, between the rams and the he goats. *Seemeth it a small thing unto you to have eaten up the good pasture, but ye must tread down with your feet the residue of your pastures? and to have drunk of the deep waters, but ye must foul the residue with your feet?* And as for my flock, they eat that which ye have trodden with your feet; and they drink that which ye have fouled with your feet. Therefore thus saith the Lord God unto them; Behold, I, even I, will judge between the fat cattle and between the lean cattle. Because ye have thrust with side and with shoulder, and pushed all the diseased with your horns, till ye have scattered them abroad; Therefore will I save my flock, and they shall no more be a prey; and I will judge between cattle and cattle.

Thus, in speaking of good and bad shepherds, the Prophet Ezekiel draws the analogy from the natural care for streams and conserving land to show what should be done in our relationships with one another. If this practical advice would be put into practice it would greatly change the concern for the environment that we struggle with today.

Many of our problems today stem from forgetting how Adam exercised his authority in Paradise. During those joyful, blessed days he lived in communion with His Creator and kept His commandments. His relationship with the animals and creation was an outgrowth of His relationship with His Creator, the Holy Trinity. He was a steward exercising this loving lordship.

A reminder that man is a steward and not the owner can be found in the both the Old and New Testaments. Moses taught the children of Israel when they had a piece of land that "the land shall not be sold in perpetuity, for the land is Mine; for in My sight you are resident aliens and sojourner (Lev. 25:23, The Orthodox Study Bible, 2008, St. Athanasius Academy Septuagint. Thomas Nelson, Inc. Nashville).

The sense of us being temporary workers and not owners is found in the Vineyard parables from the Synoptic Gospels, read during Holy Week, in the Orthodox Church. Sts. Matthew, Mark and Luke present the story of the hired workers who mistreated the servants and finally the son of the "Lord of the Vineyard."

St. Ambrose of Milan chided the Christians of his time (4th century) that began to depart from this way of stewardship. He admonishes, "Nature has poured forth all things for the common use of all men. And God has ordained that all things should be produced that there might be food in common for all. *Nature created common rights, but usurpation has transformed them into private rights.* (On the Duties of the Clergy, Book I:132. *The Nicene and Post-Nicene Fathers*, Second Series, Vol X, Eerdmans, 1989, p. 23).

In Native American history, in the speech attributed to Chief Seattle the same concerns are

"What is it that the white man wishes to buy, my people ask me? The idea is strange to us. How can you buy or sell the sky, the warmth of the land, the swiftness of the antelope? How can we sell these things to you and how can you buy them? Is the earth yours to do with as you will, merely because the red man signs a piece of paper and gives it to the white man? If we do not own the freshness of the air and the sparkle of the water, how can you buy them from us? Can you buy back the buffalo, once the last one has died?"

(*The World of Chief Seattle: How Can One Sell the Air?* Jefferson, W., 2001, p. 60. Native Voices, Book Publishing Co., Summertown, TN.)

Chief Seattle

This sense of stewardship, of hired workers, of not being the "owners" but guests, is beautifully described in one of the prayer services of the Orthodox Church known as the Akathist, "Glory to God for All Things". Written in 1940 in a communist death camp, by Protopresbyter Gregory Petrov, the second portion gracefully describes our passing through this world as thankful guests:

Kontakion 2

O Lord, how lovely it is to be Thy guest. Breeze
full of scents; mountains reaching to the skies;
waters like boundless mirrors, reflecting the sun's
golden rays and the scudding clouds. All nature
murmurs mysteriously, breathing the depth of
tenderness. Birds and beasts of the forest bear the
imprint of Thy love. Blessed art thou, mother
earth, in thy fleeting loveliness, which wakens our
yearning for happiness that will last forever, in the
land where, amid beauty that grows not old, the
cry rings out: Alleluia!

Ikos 2

Thou hast brought me into life as into an enchanted paradise. We have seen the sky like a chalice of deepest blue, where in the azure heights the birds are singing. We have listened to the soothing murmur of the forest and the melodious music of the streams. We have tasted fruit of fine flavour and the sweet-scented honey. We can live very well on Thine earth. It is a pleasure to be Thy guest.

Glory to Thee for the Feast Day of life
Glory to Thee for the perfume of lilies and roses
Glory to Thee for each different taste of berry and fruit
Glory to Thee for the sparkling silver of early morning dew
Glory to Thee for the joy of dawn's awakening
Glory to Thee for the new life each day brings
Glory to Thee, O God, from age to age.

(Retrieved from http://www.pravoslavie.ru/english/50045.htm on December 1, 2015).

What St. Justin Popovich, St. Paisios of the Holy Mountain and St Paul of Obnora were witnesses of is the very thing Orthodox Christians chant before each Sunday Liturgy during Matins in the *Songs of Ascent.* Reflect on these two for a moment:

Tone One, 2nd Antiphon: "In the Holy Spirit, all creation is made new and *hastens back to its original condition*; for He is equal in strength to the Father and the Word.

Tone Five, 3rd Antiphon: "To the Holy Spirit belongeth *the lordship of life*, for from Him every living being hath its breath, as also from the Father together with the Son."

This return to Paradise is a key aspect of our salvation. The ascetic struggle of an individual in repentance (returning) prepares the person for participating in the Divine Grace of the Son of God. This Grace of Holy Spirit is where this "lordship" is found. In the Sacramental tradition of the Orthodox

Church, there is an additional time honored way that enables the repenting community (the Church) to extend the grace of the Holy Spirit to Creation. It is found in the priestly prayers of *The Book of Needs*. They are prayers that express a sanctified Adam (*anthropos*) exercising his lordship in the earth (a return to our Paradisiacal calling). Here is one example from the *Prayer at the Sanctification of Any Fragrant Herbage*:

O Lord God Almighty, Who at Your word fills all things and commanded the earth to bring forth every fruit in its own season, and to give it for joy -- for life to man: As the same Lord, O All-gracious Master, bless and sanctify by Your Holy Spirit, this seed and various herbage brought into this holy temple, and purify from every defilement these Your servants who have received this herbage and seed, and fill their houses with every fragrance. Let it become for all who with faith preserve it and cense with it, preservation and deliverance from all increase of enemies, and for the banishment of every illusion which comes from the action of the devil, whether by day or by night, as well as for the blessing of soul and body for Your faithful people, and for the blessing of their cattle, houses, and every place. May all who receive this herbage obtain for themselves protection of soul and body, and may the mystery of Your grace be a cure for our salvation. And in whatsoever place it may be put, or by whomever it may be used, may it be for the attainment of a blessing, and may Your right hand shelter all things from which adverse powers have been driven away, to the glory of Your most-holy, majestic and all-worshiped Name: to Whom is due all glory, honor and worship, with the Father and the Holy Spirit, now and ever and unto ages of ages. Amen.

(From *Book of Needs*, 1987, p. 259, St. Tikhon's Seminary Press, South Canaan, PA)

Here is a list of other prayers from the Book of Needs revealing the synergy between the Church and nature (ibid, 1987):

The Lesser Blessing of Waters (p. 213)

Prayer Over Salt (p. 287)

Prayer Over a Sowing (p. 287)

Prayer Over a Threshing Floor [or Barn] (p. 288)

Prayer to Bless a Herd (p. 289)

Office of the Blessing of Bees (p 292)

Blessing of the Hives of an Apiary (p. 297)

Prayer to Bless New Honey (p. 298)

Prayer at the Planting of a Vineyard (p. 299)

Prayer at the Harvesting of a Vineyard (p.300)

Prayer at the Blessing of New Wine (p. 301)

Blessing of Fish for Stocking Ponds [Lakes or Rivers] (p. 302)

Order of Supplication in Time of Ruinous Pestilence of Cattle (p. 323)

What these prayers describe is an integrated way of life. The prayers of the priest are like the planting of the seeds of grace that enable man and nature to have a taste of the paradisiacal past and a foretaste of the blessed future. Indeed, they are like signposts that point the way to the life experienced by the saints.

This integrated worldview within the Orthodox Church is one of the key things that enabled the Aleut and Yupik peoples of Alaska to receive Orthodox Christianity over two hundred years ago. The following description of Fr. Michael Oleksa witnesses to this:

"A recurring theme of this volume has been the relationship between the indigenous peoples of Alaska and their land, that portion of the planet they have for centuries considered home. The Apostle Paul, St. Irenaeus of Lyons, St. Gregory of Nyssa, and St. Maximus the Confessor in ancient times, together with Pascal, Arseniev, Soloviev, Florensky and Schmemann in more recent years, have all affirmed the spiritual significance of the cosmos. This Alaskans understand. The tribes of Israel were not alone in their belief that God had given them their own promised land. Native Americans everywhere consider themselves attached to and a permanent part of their homelands, people *of* the land. Their view of the world derives from an integrated, holistic vision of reality, in which economic, social, political and artistic experiences are unified in an all-encompassing spirituality. Orthodoxy has not destroyed but enhanced this understanding. It is precisely this continuity in spiritual worldview that expedited their initial conversion to Christianity on one hand, and explains their long-term commitment to the Church on the other. Alaskan Orthodoxy reminds the Church, perhaps especially in America today, of the cosmic, integrated and therefore ecological dimensions of the Gospel" (*Orthodox Alaska*, Oleksa, M., 1992, p. 218, SVS Press, NY).

Unfortunately, the alternate view of dominion or lordship as a charter for colonizing has led to the saddest chapters in the history of our nation. The genocidal conquest of the Native Americans and the kidnapping and dehumanizing of Africans in the European Slave Trade are two indicators of such a dominion without the pursuit of the perfection spoken of by the Apostle Barnabas. A great Lakota leader, Black Elk, spoke of this in 1913. After he had become a Catholic catechist, he spoke at Sing Sing in New York:

> "You came to this country which was ours in the first place. We were the only inhabitants. After we listened to you, we settled down. But you're not doing what you're supposed to do -- what our religion and our Bible tells us. I know this. Christ himself preached that we love our neighbors as ourself. Do unto others as you would have others do unto you"
>
> (*Nicholas Black Elk: Medicine Man, Missionary, Mystic*, Steltenkamp, M. 2009, p. 106. University of Oklahoma Press: Norman, OK).

In spite of such systemic evils, grace abounded to searching souls. From being a former slave, a young George Washington Carver found the kind of Edenic lordship in the plants of Missouri and Alabama.

 "Like Adam in Paradise, young George grew up lovingly tending God's garden of plants and flowers, as well as the animals and insects of the forest, gaining wisdom and conversing with God. As he said, 'Nature in its varied forms are the little windows through which God permits me to commune with Him and to see much of His glory, majesty, and power by simply lifting up the curtain and looking in.' For his remarkable interest in and aptitude with plants, and gift for healing sick ones, he became known as the 'plant doctor' and neighbors sought his advice"

(*Wade in the River*, Altschul, P, 2001. CrossBearers Publishing, Kansas City, MO. www.stmaryofegypt.net).

Thirteen hundred years earlier, St. John of Damascus wrote, "The whole earth is a living icon of the face of God" in his *On The Divine Images*. A common

George Washington Carver

simple description for icons is that they are like 'windows of heaven.' George Washington Carver found this in nature, as St. John of Damascus said. He continued his life as a dedicated Christian who always gave glory to God.

I live in a small skete in Northwest Missouri. We are surrounded by 65-acres of forest with many trails, and 15-acres of pasture. We daily encounter deer, turkey, squirrels, possum, many birds and trees that have been here since the first European settlers came. I feel the pain that I have caused through my sins, and the magnified pain that we have brought to this region by not understanding Jesus's way of exercising Lordship, as servants and healers. I know that the way out is through a radical reversal that begins in my heart. Is it too late? Many say it is. But my hope is in the words of the Holy Prophet Joel:

"'Now, therefore,' says the Lord, 'Turn to Me with all your heart, with fasting, with weeping, and with mourning.' So rend your heart, and not your garments; return to the Lord your God, for He is gracious and merciful, slow to anger, and great kindness; and He relents from doing harm. Who knows if He will turn and relent, and leave a blessing behind Him? (*Joel 2:12-14a*, NKJV, Nelson Publishing, Inc. Nashville)

When I was on Mt. Athos I met a holy elder who wants to stay anonymous. He told me of an experience he had in the Russian forest. All alone and vulnerable, he sat praying. All of a sudden a large Grizzly bear appeared who looked very hungry, and he was coming straight for him. He quickly thought, "Well, Lord, this looks like it is my time!" As the bear came within a few feet, he gently traced the sign of the cross in front of his guest. As he was doing this, the bear stopped, and followed the movement of the cross in the air with his nose, sniffing as he moved. After that, he simply turned around and walked away! That is the kind of dominion, the exercising of Adam's lordship that the holy ones invite us to. That's the kind of love and presence the deer are waiting for. At least, let's do our part to head in that direction. Forgive me a sinner.

Unworthy Hieromonk Alexii

Made in the USA
Las Vegas, NV
01 January 2022